LIFE CYCLES
Pumpkins

by Robin Nelson

first step nonfiction

Lerner Publications Company · Minneapolis

These are pumpkins.

How do pumpkins grow?

First, **roots** grow out of the seed.

Then a **shoot** pushes up through the dirt.

Leaves grow on the **seedling**.

Each leaf grows bigger than the last one.

Next, **vines** spread out
across the ground.

Then flower **buds** grow.

The yellow flowers open.

Bees fly to the flowers.

New pumpkins start to grow
behind the flowers.

The flowers fall off, and the pumpkin grows.

The pumpkin grows big and orange.

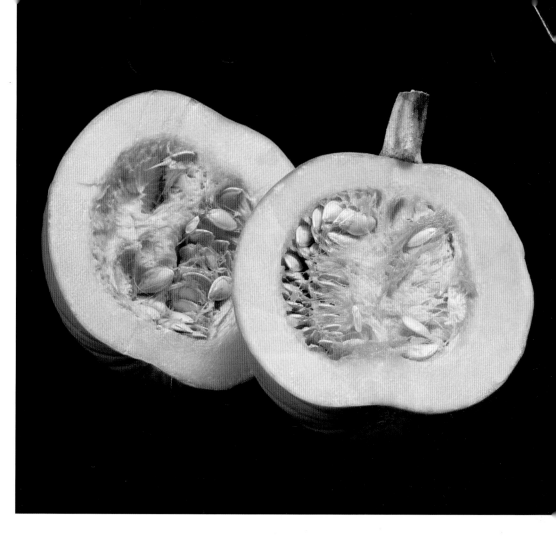

New pumpkin seeds grow
inside the pumpkin.

Some animals and people
eat pumpkin seeds.

The rest will be planted to grow new pumpkins.

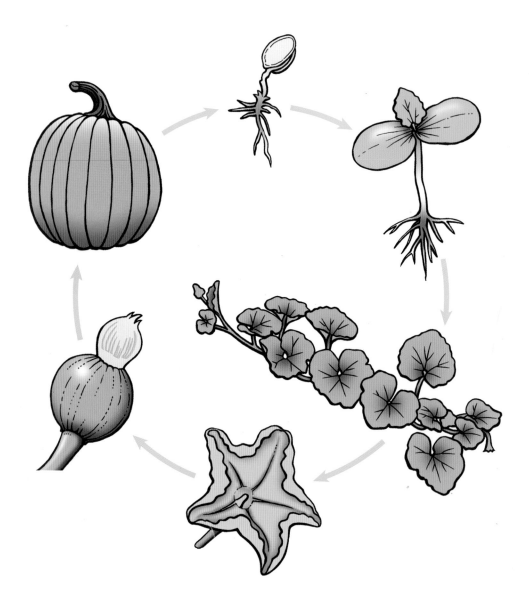

Pumpkins

Pumpkins come in many sizes and colors. Pumpkins are grown all over the world. Illinois, Ohio, Pennsylvania, and California grow the most pumpkins in the United States.

The life cycle of a pumpkin is about 120 days. This means seeds planted in the late spring are ready by October and Halloween.

Pumpkin Facts

 Pumpkin flowers close during the day and open at night.

 A pumpkin has seeds, so it is a fruit. Some people think it is a vegetable because it is not sweet.

 Pumpkin seeds are very good for you. Some people save pumpkin seeds, roast them, and then eat them. Yum!

 You can eat pumpkin flowers!

Pie, bread, and soup is made from pumpkins.

 Many people carve jack-o'-lanterns out of pumpkins for Halloween.

 Without bees, there would be no pumpkins. Bees spread pollen from flower to flower. This makes the pumpkin grow.

 A pumpkin has up to 200 seeds inside it.

Glossary

 buds – a flower that has not opened yet

 roots – parts of a plant that grow down into the ground

 seedling – a young plant

 shoot – a plant that has just started to grow

 vines – parts of a plant that grow on the ground. Some vines grow on trees and walls.

Index

The images in this book are used with the permission of: © Karlene Schwartz, pp. 2, 9, 13, 22 (top); © iStockphoto.com/archives, p. 3; © Dwight Kuhn, pp. 4, 5, 6, 11, 22 (second, third and forth from top); © Julie Caruso/Independent Picture Service, pp. 7, 10; © iStockphoto.com/Aimin Tang, p. 8; © Inga Spence/Photo Researchers, Inc., p. 12; © Inga Spence/Visuals Unlimited, Inc., p. 14; © Todd Strand/Independent Picture Service, p. 15; © Julie Caruso, p. 16; © Chris Ware/ The Image Works, p. 17; illustrations by ©Laura Westlund/Independent Picture Service. Front Cover: © iStockphoto.com/Craig Barhorst .

Lerner Publications Company
A division of Lerner Publishing Group, Inc.
241 First Avenue North
Minneapolis, MN 55401 U.S.A.

Website address: www.lernerbooks.com

Library of Congress Cataloging-in-Publication Data

Nelson, Robin, 1971–
        Pumpkins / by Robin Nelson.
            p.   cm. — (First step nonfiction. Plant life cycles)
        Includes index.
        ISBN: 978–0–7613–4073–7 (lib. bdg. : alk. paper)
            1. Pumpkin—Life cycles—Juvenile literature. I. Title. II. Series.
    SB347.N45 2009
        635'.62—dc22   2008033736

Manufactured in the United States of America
1 2 3 4 5 6 – DP – 14 13 12 11 10 09